# Composición d
# Story Writing

## Primer a Tercer Grado
## Grades 1-3

**Escrito por/Written by Ruth Solski**
**Traducido por/Translated by Hellen Martínez**
**Ilustrado por/Illustrated by S&S Learning Materials**

**ISBN 1-55035-846-4**
 "Reconocemos el apoyo financiero brindado por el Gobierno de Canadá a través del programa de Desarrollo para la Industria de Publicación de Libros (BPIDP) para este proyecto."

 "We acknowledge the financial support of the Government of Canada through the Book Publishing Industry Development Program (BPIDP) for this project."

Published in the United States by:
On the Mark Press
3909 Witmer Road PMB 175
Niagara Falls, New York
14305
www.onthemarkpress.com

Published in Canada by:
S&S Learning Materials
15 Dairy Avenue
Napanee, Ontario
K7R 1M4
www.sslearning.com

# Bilingual Workbooks in Spanish and English

## Basic Skills in Language and Mathematics for:

- ESL (English as a Second Language)
- SSL (Spanish as a Second Language)
- ELL (English Language Learners)

Congratulations on your purchase of a worthwhile learning resource! Here is a ready-to-use bilingual series for busy educators and parents. Use these workbooks to teach, review and reinforce basic skills in language and mathematics. The series' easy-to-use format provides Spanish content on the right-facing page, and the corresponding English content on the left-facing page. Comprised of curriculum-based material on reading, language and math, these workbooks are ideal for both first and second language learners.

Wherever possible, the activities in this series have been directly translated from one language to the other. This "direct translation" approach has been used with all activities featuring core skills that are the same in both Spanish and English. For the basic skills that differ between Spanish and English, an "adaptation" approach has been used. In the adapted activities, the Spanish content may be very different from the English content on the corresponding page – yet both worksheets present concepts and skills that are central to each language. By using a combination of both direct translations and adaptations of the activities, this bilingual series provides worksheets that will help children develop a solid understanding of the basic concepts in math, reading and language in both Spanish and English.

## Composición de Historias/Story Writing

*Composición de Historias/Story Writing* is an effective resource for teaching or reviewing story writing skills. The activities in this book provide practice in the following concepts: identifying the main idea, identifying a topic sentence, identifying and writing supporting details, sequencing sentences, writing descriptive, narrative and directive stories, and completing story starters with supporting details.

### Also Available

## Spanish/English Practice in...

| | | |
|---|---|---|
| OTM-2524 | • SSY1-24 | Numeración/Numeration |
| OTM-2525 | • SSY1-25 | Adición/Addition |
| OTM-2526 | • SSY1-26 | Sustracción/Subtraction |
| OTM-2527 | • SSY1-27 | Fonética/Phonics |
| OTM-2528 | • SSY1-28 | Leer para Entender/Reading for Meaning |
| OTM-2529 | • SSY1-29 | Uso de las Mayúsculas y Reglas de Puntuación/ Capitalization & Punctuation |
| OTM-2530 | • SSY1-30 | Composición de Oraciones/Sentence Writing |
| OTM-2531 | • SSY1-31 | Composición de Historias/Story Writing |

# Cuadernos de trabajo bilingües en español e inglés

## Fundamentos de lenguaje y matemática para:

- ISI (Inglés como Segundo Idioma)
- ESI (Español como Segundo Idioma)
- EII (Estudiantes de Idioma Inglés)

¡Felicitaciones por la compra de esta valiosísima fuente de aprendizaje! Aquí tiene usted una serie bilingüe para educadores y padres lista para usar. Estos libros de trabajo los puede utilizar para enseñar, revisar y reforzar las habilidades básicas de lenguaje y matemática. El formato fácil de usar de esta serie le permite hacer los mismos ejercicios en dos idiomas simultáneamente, pues presenta el contenido en español en la página derecha y el contenido equivalente en inglés en la página izquierda. Compuesto por material basado en currículos escolares en lectura, lenguaje y matemática, estos libros de trabajo son ideales para estudiantes que están aprendiendo inglés y/o español como primer o segundo idioma.

Las actividades de esta serie se han traducido del inglés al español tratando de mantener la mayor similitud posible, intentando lograr un enfoque de “traducción directa”. Este enfoque se ha mantenido en todas las actividades principales tanto en inglés como en español, y en los casos en los que no se pudo hacer una traducción directa debido a las diferencias lingüísticas, se optó por la “adaptación” de las actividades. En las actividades que han sido adaptadas, el contenido en español varía del contenido de la página correspondiente en inglés, pero, aun así, ambas hojas de trabajo mantienen los conceptos y habilidades que son centrales en cada idioma. Empleando una combinación de traducción y adaptación de las actividades, esta serie bilingüe ofrece hojas de trabajo que ayudarán a su niño a desarrollar una sólida comprensión de los conceptos básicos en matemática, lectura y lenguaje tanto en español como en inglés.

## Composición de Historias/Story Writing

*Composición de Historias/Story Writing* es un recurso efectivo para la enseñanza o estudio de cómo redactar historias. Las actividades consideradas en este libro fomentan la práctica en los siguientes conceptos: identificación de la idea principal, identificación de la oración temática, identificación y escritura de instrucciones, y conclusión de una historia con detalles sustentatorios.

## What is a paragraph?

A **paragraph** is a group of sentences that tell about the same thing.

Example:

John traveled a long way with his family to their new home in our city. He used to live in a fishing village on the West Coast. Sometimes he went out in a fishing boat.

## Tips for Writing a Paragraph

1. *Indent* the first word of the paragraph.
2. Leave a *space* between each line of writing.
3. A paragraph should have a good *beginning* or *topic* sentence. The *middle sentence* or *sentences* should be about the topic sentence. The *last* sentence should end the paragraph.
4. Each sentence in a paragraph must begin with a *capital letter* and end with a *punctuation mark*.
5. A story may be *one paragraph* or made up of *many* paragraphs.
6. A paragraph describes *one topic* or *subject*.

## ¿Qué es un párrafo?

El **párrafo** es un conjunto de oraciones que relatan un mismo asunto.

Ejemplo:

Juan viajó un largo trecho con su familia para llegar a su casa nueva en nuestra ciudad. Juan antes vivía en un pueblo pesquero de la costa occidental. Algunas veces salía a pasear en un bote pesquero.

# Consejos para escribir un párrafo

1. Haz una *sangría* en la primera oración de cada párrafo.
2. Deja un *espacio* entre cada línea.
3. Un párrafo debe tener un buen *comienzo* u oración *temática*. La *oración* u *oraciones que componen el cuerpo* del párrafo deben hablar acerca de la oración temática. La *última* oración concluye el párrafo.
4. Cada una de las oraciones que componen el párrafo deben empezar con *letra mayúscula* y terminar con un *punto*.
5. Una historia puede estar compuesta por *un párrafo* o por *muchos párrafos*.
6. Un párrafo describe *un tema* u *asunto*.

# What's the Main Idea?

**Read** each paragraph carefully.

Draw a **line** under the **main idea** in each one.

**A) Teaching Baby Bears**

A mother black bear spends two years training her cubs. The first lesson she teaches them is to climb a high tree when danger is near. Then she shows them how to catch fish in the middle of a river.

**B) Signs of Spring**

On the way to school I saw many signs of spring. Daffodils were nodding in the gardens. A mother robin was carrying grass in her beak for a nest. A gardener was planting some shrubs in a freshly dug bed. The grass was turning green.

**C) The Hidden Nest**

Beside Mr. White's boathouse by the Salmon River, a mother mallard built a large nest. It was hidden from view by leafy, low-growing bushes. In the nest she laid ten speckled eggs. Her feathers completely covered them while she sat on the nest. The color of her feathers blended with the ground making her hard to find.

**D) Dressing Up**

Last Saturday it rained all day and my little sister and I had to stay in the house. Mother let us dress up in some of her old clothes and shoes. When she wasn't watching, we used some of her lipstick. She didn't like that at all and made us wash it off.

**E) A Strange Dream**

Today, I painted a picture of a strange dream that I had last night. I was visiting a land at the bottom of the sea. Huge green weeds grew there. Trees of pink coral stretched up through the blue water. Colorful fish swam by me. When I reached out to touch them, I woke up.

**F) The Secret Place**

Emily had a secret hiding place in her house. It was in the attic. She liked to go there and play with all the toys stored in the old trunks. Sometimes she looked out the window and watched the people who lived on her street.

Skill: Locating the Main Idea in a Paragraph.

# ¿Cuál es la idea principal?

Lee cada párrafo cuidadosamente y **subraya** la **idea principal** de cada uno de ellos.

### A) Enseñando a los osos bebés

Una osa negra madre dedica dos años de su vida a adiestrar a sus crías. La primera lección que les enseña es cómo trepar un árbol cuando hay un peligro cercano. Luego les enseña cómo pescar en el medio del río.

### B) Señales del advenimiento de la primavera

Cuando iba camino a la escuela vi muchas señales del advenimiento de la primavera. Los narcisos se mecían en los jardines. Una mamá petirrojo llevaba pasto en el pico para su nido. Un jardinero estaba plantando algunos arbustos en tierra fresca. El pasto se estaba tornando verde.

### C) El nido escondido

Al lado del cobertizo del Sr. Pérez en el Río Salmón, una mamá pato había construido un gran nido. El nido se escondía tras unos arbustos pequeños y frondosos. En el nido, la mamá pato dejó diez huevos moteados. Las alas de la mamá pato cubrían completamente los huevitos cuando se posaba en el nido. El color de sus alas se confundía con la tierra, haciéndola difícil de divisar.

### D) Jugando a vestirse

El sábado pasado llovió todo el día y mi hermanita y yo tuvimos que quedarnos en casa. Mi mamá nos dejó jugar a vestirnos con algunos vestidos y zapatos suyos que ya no usaba. Cuando mi mamá no se dio cuenta, mi hermanita y yo nos pusimos un poco de su lápiz de labios. A mi mamá no le gustó nada el que usáramos su lápiz de labios e hizo que nos laváramos la cara.

### E) Un extraño sueño

Hoy hice un dibujo de un sueño muy extraño que tuve anoche. Estaba visitando una tierra que se encontraba en el fondo del mar. Allí crecían enormes algas verdes. Los árboles de coral rosado se alzaban a través del agua azul. De pronto, vi unos peces de colores que nadaban cerca de mí. Cuando intenté tocarlos, me desperté.

### F) El lugar secreto

Emilia tenía un lugar secreto donde esconderse en su casa. Este lugar secreto era el ático. A Emilia le gustaba ir al ático y jugar con todos los juguetes que estaban guardados en los viejos baúles. Algunas veces Emilia miraba a través de la ventana y veía a las personas que vivían en su calle.

Objetivo: Ubicar la idea principal en el párrafo.

# What's the Main Idea?

**Read** each paragraph carefully.
Draw a **line** under the **main idea** in each one.

**A) The First Snowfall**

On Saturday morning I looked out the window and saw snowflakes dancing about. I jumped up and down with joy. Quickly I got dressed and rushed outside. The world looked beautiful and sparkling white. Every tree was wearing a snowy coat.

**B) A Mouse Problem**

The barn mice were having a problem with the farmer's cat. He was killing many of their friends. One mouse suggested they tie a bell around the cat's neck. When the bell rang they would hear the cat coming and they would have time to get to their holes.

**C) Maple Sugar**

The maple tree only grows in North America. No one knows when people discovered that its sap could be made into maple sugar. We do know that the Native People discovered the secret long, long ago.

**D) Earthworms**

Earthworms are very small animals. There are hundreds of them in the soil. They move the soil as they go through the ground. After a rain, they come to the top of the ground where robins stand, waiting to catch them.

**E) Trolls**

There are many kinds of trolls. Some live in the water while others live deep in the mountains of Norway. Trolls are usually very ugly and have eyes as big as saucers. Some trolls are small while others are as big as giants.

**F) Spider Silk**

A spider web is made of silk by the female spider. She can make five or six different kinds of silk. Some are smooth and some are different colors. A spider uses one kind of silk for trapping insects, another kind for wrapping eggs and a different kind for running along to catch trapped insects.

Skill: Locating the Main idea in a Paragraph

# ¿Cuál es la idea principal?

**Lee** cada párrafo cuidadosamente y **subraya** la **idea principal** de cada uno de ellos.

## A) La primera nieve

El sábado en la mañana miré por la ventana y vi que caían copos de nieve. Salté y salté de alegría. Me vestí rápidamente y salí corriendo a la calle. El mundo se veía hermoso y brillantemente blanco. Cada árbol estaba cubierto de nieve.

## B) Problema de ratones

Los ratones del establo tenían un problema con el gato del granjero. El gato estaba matando a muchos de sus amigos. Un ratón sugirió atar una campana alrededor del cuello del gato. Cuando la campana suene, los ratones escucharían acercarse al gato y tendrían tiempo de meterse en sus ratoneras.

## C) Azúcar de arce

El árbol de arce sólo crece en América del Norte. Nadie sabe cuándo se descubrió que con su savia se podía hacer azúcar de arce. Lo único que sabemos es que los nativos de la región descubrieron el secreto hace mucho, mucho tiempo.

## D) Lombrices de tierra

Las lombrices de tierra son unos animales muy pequeños. Hay cientos de lombrices de tierra en el suelo. Las lombrices de tierra remueven el suelo mientras se van desplazando por la tierra. Después de una lluvia, las lombrices salen a la superficie, donde los petirrojos esperan para atraparlas.

## E) Duendes

Existen muchos tipos de duendes. Algunos duendes viven en el agua, mientras que otros viven en las profundidades de las montañas noruegas. Por lo general, los duendes son muy feos y tienen los ojos tan grandes como platos. Algunos son pequeños, y otros son tan grandes como gigantes.

## F) Seda de araña

La tela de araña está hecha de una seda elaborada por la araña hembra. La araña hembra puede hacer hasta cinco o seis diferentes tipos de seda. Algunas sedas son suaves y otras son de diferentes colores. La araña usa un tipo de seda para atrapar insectos, otro tipo para envolver sus huevos y otro tipo para caminar sobre ellas y capturar a los insectos atrapados.

Objetivo: Ubicar la idea principal en el párrafo.

# What is the Topic Sentence?

A **topic sentence** is the beginning sentence of a paragraph. It tells the **main idea**.

**Read** the details in each box below. Find the **best** topic sentence. **Print** it on the lines provided.

*Picking apples is fun.*
*The beavers were busy cutting down trees.*
*Goldfish are easy to look after.*
*During recess the girls played games.*
*The wind likes to play tricks in the fall.*
*Hockey is a good game to play.*

| | |
|---|---|
| 1. take a hockey stick<br>shoot at the net<br>scored a goal<br>everyone cheers<br>____________________<br>____________________ | 3. rake the leaves<br>make three piles<br>wind comes along<br>leaves fly about<br>____________________<br>____________________ |
| 2. at the farm<br>picked some apples<br>put them in a basket<br>ate a big red one<br>____________________<br>____________________ | 4. empty the bowl<br>put the fish in a dish<br>clean the stones<br>add fresh water<br>____________________<br>____________________ |

Skill: Locating the Topic Sentence to Match the Supporting Details

# ¿Qué es la oración temática?

La **oración temática** es la primera oración del párrafo que dice la **idea principal.**

**Lee** los detalles de cada uno de los recuadros de abajo. Luego, ubica la **mejor** oración temática que concuerde con los detalles. **Escribe** la oración temática en las líneas en blanco de cada recuadro.

*Recolectar manzanas es divertido.*
*Los castores estaban ocupados talando árboles.*
*Los peces son fáciles de cuidar.*
*Las niñas jugaban durante el recreo.*
*Al viento le gusta jugarnos trucos en el otoño.*
*El hockey es un juego entretenido.*

| | |
|---|---|
| **1.** tomar un palo de hockey<br>tirar a la red<br>hacer un gol<br>todos vitorean<br>______________________<br>______________________ | **3.** rastrillar las hojas<br>hacer tres pilas de hojas<br>el viento viene<br>las hojas salen volando<br>______________________<br>______________________ |
| **2.** en la granja<br>recolectar manzanas<br>colocarlas en una canasta<br>comer una gran manzana roja<br>______________________<br>______________________ | **4.** vaciar la pecera<br>poner el pez en un plato<br>limpiar las piedras<br>colocar agua fresca<br>______________________<br>______________________ |

Objetivo: Ubicar la oración temática que concuerde con los detalles sustentatorios dados.

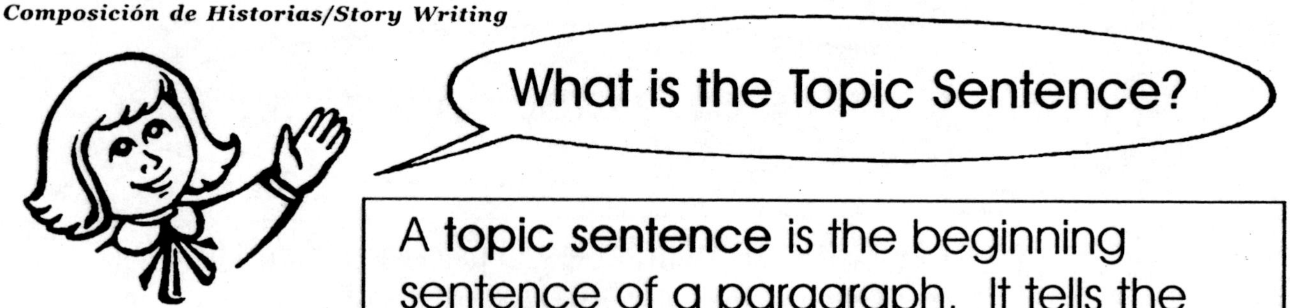


A **topic sentence** is the beginning sentence of a paragraph. It tells the **main idea.**

**Read** the details in each box below. Find the **best** topic sentence. **Print** it on the lines provided.

*Once there was an old school bus.*
*I love to play hopscotch at recess.*
*A skunk is about the size of a house cat.*
*The boys were playing baseball in the park.*
*The chickadee is a tiny, gray bird.*
*A raccoon uses its paws like a person.*

| | |
|---|---|
| **1.** small ears and eyes<br>good hearing<br>cannot see well<br>black with a white stripe<br>____________________<br>____________________ | **3.** black cap and bib<br>loves the winter<br>sings chick-a-dee-dee<br>eats suet and seeds<br>____________________<br>____________________ |
| **2.** holds food in its paws<br>rinses the food in water<br>food easier to eat<br>hunts at night<br>____________________<br>____________________ | **4.** no one drives it any more<br>cries all day long<br>feels lonely<br>misses the children<br>____________________<br>____________________ |

Skill: Locating the Topic Sentence to Match the Supporting Details

## ¿Qué es la oración temática?

La **oración temática** es la primera oración del párrafo que dice la **idea principal**.

**Lee** los detalles de cada uno de los recuadros de abajo. Luego, ubica la **mejor** oración temática que concuerde con los detalles. **Escribe** la oración temática en las líneas al final de cada recuadro.

*Había una vez un viejo autobús escolar.*
*Me encanta jugar al avión en el recreo.*
*El zorrillo es casi del tamaño de un gato.*
*Los niños estaban jugando béisbol en el parque.*
*El paro es un ave pequeñita de color gris.*
*El mapache utiliza sus patas como si fuera una persona.*

1. orejas y ojos pequeños
   buen sentido del oído
   no puede ver bien
   es negro con una raya blanca

2. sostiene la comida con sus patas
   enjuaga la comida en el agua
   la comida es más fácil de comer
   caza durante la noche

3. penacho y pecho negros
   le encanta el invierno
   canta chi-ca-di-dí
   come grasa de pella y semillas

4. ya nadie lo conduce
   llora todo el día
   se siente solo
   extraña a los niños

Objetivo: Ubicar la oración temática que concuerde con los detalles sustentatorios dados.

# Write a Topic Sentence

**Read** the details listed in each box carefully. Then **write** a good topic sentence on the lines provided.

**Details:** flies during the day
visits flower gardens
yellow and black
fuzzy and fat

**Topic Sentence:**

___

___

**Details:** place the lights on branches
wind the garland around the tree
hang the decorations
turn on the lights

**Topic Sentence:**

___

___

**Details:** leathery wings
furry body
fly at night
catch small insects

**Topic Sentence:**

___

___

Skill: Writing a Topic Sentence that Matches the Given Details

# Escribe una oración temática

**Lee** cuidadosamente los detalles que se presentan en cada recuadro. Luego **escribe** una buena oración temática en las líneas en blanco.

**Detalles:** vuela durante el día
visita los jardines de flores
es de color amarillo y negro
zumba y es rechoncha

**Oración temática:**

______________________________

______________________________

**Detalles:** cuelgan las luces en las ramas del árbol
adornan con guirnaldas el árbol
colocan las decoraciones
encienden las luces

**Oración temática:**

______________________________

______________________________

**Detalles:** alas ásperas
cuerpo peludo
vuela en las noches
caza insectos pequeños

**Oración temática:**

______________________________

______________________________

Objetivo: Componer una oración temática que concuerde con los detalles dados.

# Supporting Details

Sometimes boys and girls put too many details in their stories that are not about the topic sentence.

**Read** each paragraph carefully. **Underline** the sentence that does not belong.

### A) My Pet

Goldie is my pet goldfish. I watch him swim around the bowl. He does not seem to get dizzy. My dog can run fast too. When I drop food into the water, Goldie is very excited and swims in every direction.

### B) The Coming of Spring

In the spring, warm rain falls and the sun shines brightly in the sky. Many living things begin to move about and grow. The trees lose their leaves. The sap flows in the trees. Flowers smile and nod in the flower beds.

### C) The Birthday Party

Kelly's birthday party was on Friday after school. She had invited some of her friends. The table was decorated with yellow flowers and place cards. Her cake had nine candles. I took my dog for a long walk. We played games and sang songs.

### D) Feeding Our Winter Birds

Our classroom is close to a steep hill with bushes and evergreen trees. It is a good place to watch birds. On the window sill we put bird seed, crumbs, suet and dried corn. We enjoy watching the beavers cut down the trees. Cardinals, bluejays and chickadees come to our feeder.

### E) How Owls Hunt

Owls use their feet to catch food. Crows like to eat corn. Their feet are strong with very sharp claws. Owls hunt after the sun goes down. They fly near the gorund looking for small animals. When they see an animal, they fly down and catch it with their strong feet.

### F) Looking for Food

Father Robin was looking for food. First he put his head to one side. Then he put his head to the other side. Fluffy was Betty's pet kitten. He could hear the worms moving about under the ground. Suddenly a worm pushed its head out of a hole. Robin quickly grabbed it.

Skill: Identifyling Details That Do Not Belong

# Detalles sustentatorios

Algunas veces tendemos a colocar demasiados detalles en nuestros cuentos que no están relacionados con la oración temática.

**Lee** cuidadosamente cada párrafo y luego **subraya** la oración que no pertenece al tema.

### A) Mi mascota

Mi mascota es un pececito que se llama Goldie. Me gusta mirarlo nadar en su pecera. Pareciera que nunca se mareara. Mi perro también puede correr rápido. Cuando pongo comida en el agua, Goldie se emociona mucho y nada por todos lados.

### B) El advenimiento de la primavera

En la primavera, cae una lluvia tibia y el sol brilla resplandeciente en el cielo. Muchos seres vivientes comienzan a moverse y a crecer. Los árboles pierden sus hojas. La sábila fluye en los árboles. Las flores sonríen y se mecen en los jardines.

### C) La fiesta de cumpleaños

La fiesta de cumpleaños de Anita fue el viernes después de la escuela. Anita había invitado a algunos de sus amigos. La mesa estaba decorada con flores amarillas y tarjetitas. Su pastel tenía nueve velas. Llevé a mi perro a dar un largo paseo. Participamos en varios juegos y cantamos mucho.

### D) Alimentando a nuestras aves en invierno

Nuestro salón de clases está cerca de una colina que tiene arbustos y árboles perennes. Es un buen lugar para observar pájaros. En el umbral de la ventana, ponemos semillas, terrones, grasa de pella y maíz seco. Disfrutamos ver a los castores cortando los árboles. Nuestro comedero se llena de cardinales, urracas y paros.

### E) Cómo cazan las lechuzas

Las lechuzas usan sus patas para agarrar comida. A los cuervos les gusta comer maíz. Sus patas son fuertes y tienen garras muy filudas. Las lechuzas cazan al ponerse el sol. Vuelan cerca de la tierra buscando animales pequeños. Cuando ven un animal, vuelan hacia él y lo atrapan con sus poderosas garras.

### F) Buscando comida

El petirrojo papá andaba buscado comida. Primero dirigió su cabeza hacia un lado. Luego dirigió su cabeza hacia el otro. Minino era el gatito de Beatriz. Podía escuchar a las lombrices moviéndose debajo de la tierra. De pronto, una lombriz asomó su cabeza fuera de un agujero. El petirrojo rápidamente lo agarró.

Objetivo: Identificar los detalles que no pertenecen al tema.

# Writing Supporting Details

**Read** the main idea sentence. Write **four** supporting details.

I love buttermilk pancakes.

1. ______________________________
2. ______________________________
3. ______________________________
4. ______________________________

Girls make good hockey players.

1. ______________________________
2. ______________________________
3. ______________________________
4. ______________________________

Skill: Brainstorming and Recording Supporting Details

# Composición de detalles sustentatorios

**Lee** la oración de la idea principal. Luego escribe **cuatro** detalles sustentatorios.

## Me encantan los panqués con crema.

1. ____________________
2. ____________________
3. ____________________
4. ____________________

## Las niñas son buenas jugadoras de hockey.

1. ____________________
2. ____________________
3. ____________________
4. ____________________

Objetivo: Dar ideas y escribir detalles sustentatorios.

# Writing Supporting Details

**Read** the main idea sentence. Write **four** supporting details.

The hippopotamus is often called "the river horse".

1. ____________________
2. ____________________
3. ____________________
4. ____________________

My mother taught me how to make my bed.

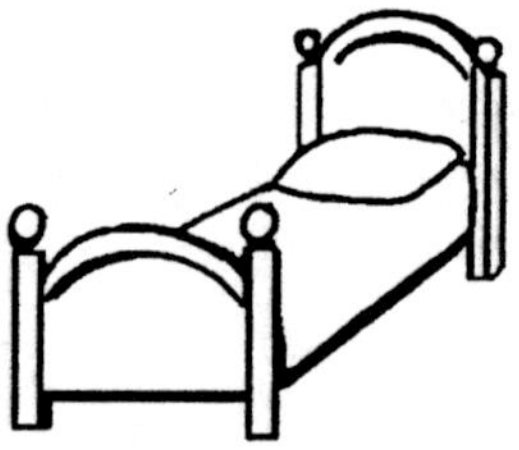

1. ____________________
2. ____________________
3. ____________________
4. ____________________

Skill: Brainstorming and Recording Supporting Details

# Composición de detalles sustentatorios

**Lee** la oración de la idea principal. Luego escribe **cuatro** detalles sustentatorios.

## El hipopótamo también es conocido como el "caballo de río".

1. ______________________________
2. ______________________________
3. ______________________________
4. ______________________________

## Mi mamá me enseñó a tender mi cama.

1. ______________________________
2. ______________________________
3. ______________________________
4. ______________________________

Objetivo: Dar ideas y escribir detalles sustentatorios.

# Sequencing Sentences

Sentences in a paragraph or story are written in a certain order so they make sense.

**Number** the sentences, in each box, in the correct order to tell a story. Use the numerals **1, 2, 3, 4.**

A)

_____ The third Billy Goat Gruff butted the troll off the bridge.
_____ The ugly troll wouldn't let anyone cross his bridge.
_____ The three Billy Goats Gruff wanted to cross the bridge.
_____ The first and second Billy Goat Gruff tricked the troll and crossed the bridge.

B)

_____ The Hare took off quickly and was so far ahead of the Tortoise, he decided to have a little rest.
_____ When the Hare woke up he saw the Tortoise crossing the finish line.
_____ The Hare was always making fun of the slow way the Tortoise moved, so they decided to have a race.
_____ The Tortoise passed the Hare as he slept.

C)

_____ Goldilocks broke Little Bear's chair and fell asleep in his bed.
_____ She ate all of Little Bear's porridge.
_____ The Three Bears came home and frightened her.
_____ Goldilocks went into the Bears' house to look around.

Skill: Sequencing Sentences in the Correct Order

# Oraciones de enlace

Las oraciones de un párrafo o una historia se deben escribir siguiendo cierto orden, de tal manera que tengan sentido.

En cada uno de los siguientes recuadros, **enumera** las oraciones en el orden correcto para contar una historia. Emplea los números 1, 2, 3 y 4.

A)

_______ El tercer Macho Cabrío embistió al duende, lanzándolo por el puente.

_______ Un horrible duende no dejaba que nadie cruzara su puente.

_______ El tercer Macho Cabrío quería cruzar el puente.

_______ El primer y el segundo Macho Cabrío burlaron al duende y pudieron cruzar el puente.

B)

_______ La Liebre partió rápidamente y en poco tiempo ya estaba bastante lejos de la Tortuga, así que decidió tomar un pequeño descanso.

_______ Cuando la Liebre despertó, vio que la Tortuga ya estaba cruzando la meta.

_______ La Liebre siempre se burlaba de lo lento que caminaba la Tortuga, así que decidieron hacer una carrera.

_______ Mientras la Liebre dormía, la Tortuga la pasó.

C)

_______ Ricitos de Oro rompió la silla del Osito y se quedó dormida en su cuna.

_______ Se comió todo el potaje del Osito.

_______ Los Tres Osos regresaron a su casa y la asustaron.

_______ Ricitos de Oro entró a la casa de los osos para curiosear.

Objetivo: Unir las oraciones en secuencia, en el orden correcto.

# Sequencing Sentences

**Sentences in a paragraph or story are written in a certain order so they make sense.**

Copy each group of sentences in the correct order to make a story or a paragraph. Print them neatly on the lines provided.

**A)**

Mother Robin laid three blue eggs in the nest.
Soon, three baby robins hatched from the eggs.
She sat on the eggs to keep them warm.
The robins were very busy building a nest of twigs and grass.

______________________________________________

______________________________________________

______________________________________________

______________________________________________

______________________________________________

______________________________________________

**B)**

Finally, Paul was on his way to school.
Then he ate his breakfast.
Paul's alarm clock rang and woke him up.
He got up and got dressed quickly.

______________________________________________

______________________________________________

______________________________________________

______________________________________________

______________________________________________

______________________________________________

Skill: Sequencing Sentences to Create a Story or a Paragraph

# Oraciones de enlace

**Las oraciones de un párrafo o una historia se deben escribir siguiendo cierto orden, de tal manera que tengan sentido.**

Copia cada grupo de oraciones que están en los recuadros en el orden correcto para crear una historia o un párrafo. Escribe claramente en las líneas de abajo.

**A)**

La Mamá Petirrojo dejó tres huevos azules en el nido.
En poco tiempo, salieron tres petirrojos bebés de los cascarones.
Se sentó sobre los huevos para mantenerlos calientes.
Los petirrojos estaban muy ocupados construyendo su nido con ramitas y pasto.

**B)**

Finalmente, Pablo se puso de camino a la escuela.
Luego tomó desayuno.
La alarma de Pablo sonó y él se despertó.
Se levantó y se vistió rápidamente.

Objetivo: Enlazar oraciones para crear una historia o un párrafo.

# Writing a Descriptive Story

## My Favorite Food

I love to eat ______________________________

______________________________

(Describe how it looks.)

______________________________

(Describe how it smells.)

______________________________

______________________________

(Describe how its tastes.)

______________________________

Write another paragraph about the food you hate to eat. Follow the same pattern. Underline your topic sentence.

______________________________

______________________________

______________________________

______________________________

______________________________

______________________________

______________________________

______________________________

______________________________

Skill: Developing a Descriptive Story Using a Model.

# Composición de una historia descriptiva

## Mi comida favorita

Me encanta comer ______________________________

______________________________

(Describe su apariencia.)

______________________________

(Describe su olor.)

______________________________

______________________________

(Describe su sabor.)

______________________________

Escribe otro párrafo que hable sobre la comida que no te gusta comer. Sigue el mismo orden. Subraya tu oración temática.

______________________________

______________________________

______________________________

______________________________

______________________________

______________________________

______________________________

______________________________

Objetivo: Desarrollar una historia descriptiva utilizando un modelo.

# Writing a Descriptive Story

## My Favorite Toy

I love to play with ______________________________

______________________________

(Describe how it looks.)

______________________________

(Describe how it moves or works.)

______________________________

______________________________

______________________________

(Describe how it feels.)

______________________________

______________________________

______________________________

Write about another toy that you like to play with. Follow the same pattern. Underline your topic sentence.

______________________________

______________________________

______________________________

______________________________

______________________________

______________________________

Skill: Developing a Descriptive Story Using a Model.

# Composición de una historia descriptiva

## Mi juguete favorito

Me encanta jugar con ________________________________

________________________________________________

(Describe su apariencia.)

________________________________________________

(Describe cómo se mueve o cómo funciona.)

________________________________________________

________________________________________________

________________________________________________

(Describe qué sientes con tu juguete.)

________________________________________________

________________________________________________

________________________________________________

Escribe acerca de otro juguete con el que también te guste jugar. Sigue el mismo orden. Subraya tu oración temática.

________________________________________________

________________________________________________

________________________________________________

________________________________________________

________________________________________________

________________________________________________

Objetivo: Desarrollar una historia descriptiva utilizando un modelo.

# Writing a Descriptive Story

## My Best Friend

My best friend is ______________________________

(Describe how your friend looks.)

______________________________

______________________________

(Describe the things you do together.)

______________________________

______________________________

______________________________

(Tell why he/she is your best friend.)

______________________________

______________________________

Write about a relative in your family that you really like. It may be an aunt, uncle, grandparent or cousin. Follow the same pattern. Underline your topic sentence.

______________________________

______________________________

______________________________

______________________________

______________________________

______________________________

______________________________

Skill: Developing a Descriptive Story Using a Model.

# Composición de una historia descriptiva

## Mi mejor amigo(a)

Mi mejor amigo(a) es ________________________________

________________________________________________

(Describe la apariencia de tu mejor amigo(a).)

________________________________________________

________________________________________________

(Describe las cosas que les gusta hacer juntos.)

________________________________________________

________________________________________________

________________________________________________

(Explica por qué es tu mejor amigo(a).)

________________________________________________

________________________________________________

Escribe acerca de algún miembro de tu familia al que realmente quieras mucho. Puede ser un tío, una tía, un abuelo, una abuela, un primo o una prima. Sigue el mismo orden. Subraya tu oración temática.

________________________________________________

________________________________________________

________________________________________________

________________________________________________

________________________________________________

________________________________________________

Objetivo: Desarrollar una historia descriptiva utilizando un modelo.

# Writing a Narrative Story

## My Happiest Day

Have you ever been so happy you felt like you would explode if you didn't tell someone what had happened?

I felt that way ______________________________

______________________________

______________________________

So I ran to tell ______________________________

because ______________________________

______________________________

______________________________

Describe the time when you felt so angry that you wanted to scream. Follow the pattern or try to write your own story. Remember to use a topic sentence and two or three supporting details.

______________________________

______________________________

______________________________

______________________________

______________________________

______________________________

______________________________

______________________________

Skill: Developing a Narrative Story Using a Model.

# Composición de una historia narrativa

## El día más feliz de mi vida

¿Alguna vez has estado tan contento que sentías que ibas a explotar si no le decías a alguien lo que te pasó?

Una vez me sentí así, cuando ______________________________

____________________________________________________________

____________________________________________________________

Así que corrí a decírselo a ______________________________

porque ______________________________________________________

____________________________________________________________

____________________________________________________________

Describe la vez que te hayas sentido tan enojado que hayas querido gritar. Sigue el mismo orden o trata de escribir tu propia historia. Recuerda: utiliza una oración temática y dos o tres detalles sustentatorios.

____________________________________________________________

____________________________________________________________

____________________________________________________________

____________________________________________________________

____________________________________________________________

____________________________________________________________

____________________________________________________________

____________________________________________________________

Objetivo: Desarrollar una historia narrativa utilizando un modelo.

# Writing a Narrative Story

## My Perfect Day

Yesterday was the most perfect day of my life. I felt great. It began when ______________________________

______________________________

Then ______________________________

______________________________

The best part was when ______________________________

______________________________

______________________________

Write a paragraph about the worst day of your life.
Follow the same pattern. Underline the topic sentence.
Remember to write two or three supporting details.

______________________________

______________________________

______________________________

______________________________

______________________________

______________________________

______________________________

Skill: Developing a Narrative Story Using a Pattern.

# Composición de una historia narrativa

## Mi día perfecto

Ayer fue el día más perfecto de mi vida. Me sentía de lo mejor.

Todo comenzó cuando ______________________________

Luego ______________________________

______________________________

La mejor parte fue cuando ______________________________

______________________________

______________________________

______________________________

Escribe un párrafo acerca del peor día de tu vida. Sigue el mismo orden. Subraya las oraciones temáticas. Recuerda: escribe dos o tres detalles sustentatorios.

______________________________

______________________________

______________________________

______________________________

______________________________

______________________________

______________________________

Objetivo: Desarrollar una historia narrativa utilizando un modelo.

# Writing a Narrative Story

## Penguins

In my opinion the most interesting birds are

______________________________________________

______________________________________________

(Give three or more reasons.)

______________________________________________

______________________________________________

______________________________________________

______________________________________________

______________________________________________

______________________________________________

Write another paragraph about any animal or bird. Remember to use a good topic sentence and three or more supporting details.

______________________________________________

______________________________________________

______________________________________________

______________________________________________

______________________________________________

______________________________________________

______________________________________________

Skill: Developing a Narrative Story Independently.

# Composición de una historia narrativa

## Pingüinos

En mi opinión, las aves más interesantes son

________________________________________

________________________________________

(Da tres o más razones del por qué piensas que son interesantes.)

________________________________________

________________________________________

________________________________________

________________________________________

________________________________________

________________________________________

Escribe otro párrafo acerca de cualquier otro animal o ave. Recuerda: utiliza una buena oración temática y tres o más detalles sustentatorios.

________________________________________

________________________________________

________________________________________

________________________________________

________________________________________

________________________________________

________________________________________

Objetivo: Escribir una historia narrativa de manera independiente.

# Writing Directions

## Building a Snowman

In the winter I like to build a snowman.

First, I ______________________________

______________________________

______________________________

Second, I ______________________________

______________________________

Third, I ______________________________

______________________________

Last of all, I ______________________________

______________________________

______________________________

Draw a picture in each box to show the steps you took.

| | |
|---|---|
| | |
| | |

Skill: Writing a Directive Paragraph and Illustrating It.

# Composición de instrucciones

## Cómo hacer un hombre de nieve

Cuando llega el invierno, me gusta salir a hacer un hombre de nieve.

Primero, ______________________________________________

______________________________________________

______________________________________________

Segundo, ______________________________________________

______________________________________________

Tercero, ______________________________________________

______________________________________________

______________________________________________

Finalmente, ______________________________________________

Dibuja una figura en cada cuadro para mostrar los pasos que seguiste para hacer el hombre de nieve.

| | |
|---|---|
| | |
| | |

Objetivo: Escribir un párrafo de instrucciones e ilustrarlo.

# Writing Directions

## Carving a Jack-'o-lantern

At Halloween I always make a jack-'o-lantern.

I go to a farm to get a ______________________________

First, I ______________________________

______________________________

Second, I ______________________________

______________________________

Third, I ______________________________

______________________________

Last of all, I ______________________________

______________________________

Draw a picture in each box to show the steps you took.

| | |
|---|---|
| | |
| | |

Skill: Writing a Directive Paragraph.

# Composición de instrucciones

## Cómo hacer una linterna de calabaza para el Día de Brujas

En el Día de las Brujas siempre hago una linterna de calabaza. Voy a una granja para comprar una ______________

Primero, ____________________________________________

______________________________________________________

Segundo, ____________________________________________

______________________________________________________

Tercero, ____________________________________________

______________________________________________________

Finalmente, __________________________________________

______________________________________________________

Dibuja una figura en cada cuadro para mostrar los pasos que seguiste para hacer la linterna de calabaza.

Objetivo: Escribir un párrafo de instrucciones e ilustrarlo.

# Writing Directions

## Making Valentine Cards

For my friends on Valentine's Day, I like to make Valentine cards. I get colored paper, lacy doilies, crayons, glue and scissors.

First, I ______________________________

______________________________

Second, I ______________________________

______________________________

Third, I ______________________________

______________________________

Last of all, I ______________________________

______________________________

Draw a picture in each box to show the steps you took.

| | |
|---|---|
| | |
| | |

Skill: Writing a Directive Paragraph.

# Composición de instrucciones

## Cómo hacer tarjetas de San Valentín

En el día de San Valentín me gusta hacer tarjetas de San Valentín para mis amigos. Busco papeles de colores, servilletas de filigrana, crayones, pegamento y tijeras.

Primero, ______________________________________

______________________________________________

Segundo, ______________________________________

______________________________________________

Tercero, ______________________________________

______________________________________________

Finalmente, ___________________________________

______________________________________________

Dibuja una figura en cada cuadro para mostrar los pasos que seguiste para hacer las tarjetas de San Valentín.

| | |
|---|---|
| | |
| | |

Objetivo: Escribir un párrafo de instrucciones e ilustrarlo.

## Writing a Story

Complete the story starter with supporting details.

If I were a fairy, I would fly around the world helping people.

---

## Writing a Story

Complete the story starter with supporting details.

If I were a pirate, I would sail around the world looking for treasure.

Skill: Writing Details to Support a Topic Sentence.

## Composición de una historia

Completa el inicio de la historia con detalles sustentatorios.

Si yo fuera un hada, volaría por todo el mundo ayudando a la gente.

## Composición de una historia

Completa el inicio de la historia con detalles sustentatorios.

Si yo fuera un pirata, navegaría por todo el mundo buscando tesoros.

Objetivo: Escribir detalles para sustentar la oración temática.

## Writing a Story

Complete the story starter with supporting details.

One night I had the most delicious dream. I dreamt of ______________________________

______________________________

______________________________

______________________________

______________________________

______________________________

______________________________

______________________________

______________________________

## Writing a Story

Complete the story starter with supporting details.

My dog was black and dirty from playing in the mud. I decided to ______________________________

______________________________

______________________________

______________________________

______________________________

______________________________

______________________________

______________________________

______________________________

______________________________

Skill: Writing Details to Support a Topic Sentence.

## Composición de una historia

Completa el inicio de la historia con detalles sustentatorios.

Una noche, tuve el más delicioso de los sueños. Soñé que ______________________________

## Composición de una historia

Completa el inicio de la historia con detalles sustentatorios.

Mi perro regresó negro y sucio después de haber jugado en el fango. Decidí ______________________________

Objetivo: Escribir detalles para sustentar la oración temática.

## Writing a Story

Complete the story starter with supporting details.

Once upon a time there was a turtle who loved to play baseball. Timothy Turtle ______________________

---

## Writing a Story

Complete the story starter with supporting details.

Once upon a time there lived a mouse who liked to eat cheese and other good things. One day the mouse

Skill: Writing Details to Support a Topic Sentence.

## Composición de una historia

Completa el inicio de la historia con detalles sustentatorios.

Había una vez una tortuga a la que le gustaba mucho jugar al béisbol. La Tortuga Timoteo ____________________

______________________________________________________
______________________________________________________
______________________________________________________
______________________________________________________
______________________________________________________
______________________________________________________
______________________________________________________
______________________________________________________

## Composición de una historia

Completa el inicio de la histsoria con detalles sustentatorios.

Había una vez un ratón a quien le gustaba mucho comer queso y otras cosas sabrosas. Un día el ratón __________

______________________________________________________
______________________________________________________
______________________________________________________
______________________________________________________
______________________________________________________
______________________________________________________
______________________________________________________
______________________________________________________
______________________________________________________

Objetivo: Escribir detalles para sustentar la oración temática.

## Writing a Story

Complete the story starter with supporting details.

Once upon a time there was a grand castle sitting at the top of Windy Hill. In the castle lived

## Writing a Story

Complete the story starter with supporting details.

In a cave, outside of town, lived a terrible dragon. No one could get near him because

Skill: Writing Details to Support a Topic Sentence.

## Composición de una historia

Completa el inicio de la historia con detalles sustentatorios.

Había una vez un enorme castillo que se encontraba en lo alto de la Colina de Vientos. En el castillo vivía

________________________________________

________________________________________

________________________________________

________________________________________

________________________________________

________________________________________

________________________________________

________________________________________

---

## Composición de una historia

Completa el inicio de la historia con detalles sustentatorios.

En una cueva lejana, en las afueras del pueblo, vivía un horrible dragón. Nadie podía acercársele porque ______________________________

________________________________________

________________________________________

________________________________________

________________________________________

________________________________________

________________________________________

________________________________________

________________________________________

________________________________________

Objetivo: Escribir detalles para sustentar la oración temática.

## Writing a Story

Complete the story starter with supporting details.

In the attic of an old house lived a little ghost called Gloria. Sometimes she could be seen floating by the windows. Sometimes ______________________________

________________________________________

________________________________________

________________________________________

________________________________________

________________________________________

________________________________________

________________________________________

## Writing a Story

Complete the story starter with supporting details.

Ella the elephant was a famous circus star. She was known all over the world for ______________________

________________________________________

________________________________________

________________________________________

________________________________________

________________________________________

________________________________________

________________________________________

________________________________________

________________________________________

Skill: Writing Details to Support a Topic Sentence.

## Composición de una historia

Completa el inicio de la historia con detalles sustentatorios.

En el ático de una vieja casona vivía una pequeña fantasmita llamada Gloria. Algunas veces se podía ver a Gloria flotando a través de las ventanas. Otras, Gloria ______________________________

______________________________

______________________________

______________________________

______________________________

______________________________

______________________________

---

## Composición de una historia

Completa el inicio de la historia con detalles sustentatorios.

La elefanta Elena era una famosa estrella de circo. Se le conocía por todo el mundo por su ____________

______________________________

______________________________

______________________________

______________________________

______________________________

______________________________

______________________________

______________________________

______________________________

Objetivo: Escribir detalles para sustentar la oración temática.

## Writing a Story

Complete the story starter with supporting details.

The children were playing happily at the beach. They were ______________________________

---

## Writing a Story

Complete the story starter with supporting details.

It was clean-up week. Becky and Brad were helping to clean up ______________________

Skill: Writing Details to Support a Topic Sentence.

## Composición de una historia

Completa el inicio de la historia con detalles sustentatorios.

Los niños jugaban alegremente en la playa. Ellos estaban ______________________

---

## Composición de una historia

Completa el inicio de la historia con detalles sustentatorios.

Era la semana de limpieza. Rebeca y Roberto ayudaban a limpiar ______________

Objetivo: Escribir detalles para sustentar la oración temática.

## Writing a Story

Complete the story starter with supporting details.

Many years ago dinosaurs roamed our land. Some were plant-eaters while others were meat-eaters. Dinosaurs ______________________

---

## Writing a Story

Complete the story starter with supporting details.

The giraffe is the tallest mammal in the world. It has ______________________

Skill: Writing Details to Support a Topic Sentence.

## Composición de una historia

Completa el inicio de la historia con detalles sustentatorios.

Hace mucho años, los dinosaurios habitaban nuestra tierra. Algunos dinosaurios eran herbívoros, mientras otros eran carnívoros. Los dinosaurios

## Composición de una historia

Completa el inicio de la historia con detalles sustentatorios.

La jirafa es el mamífero más alto del mundo. Tiene

Objetivo: Escribir detalles para sustentar la oración temática.

## Writing a Story

Complete the story starter with supporting details.

Joey was going to make pancakes for breakfast. First, he ______________________________

---

## Writing a Story

Complete the story starter with supporting details.

Martin was at the painting center. First, he ______________________________

Skills: Writing Details to Support a Topic Sentence.

## Composición de una historia

Completa el inicio de la historia con detalles sustentatorios.

José iba a hacer panqués para el desayuno.

Primero, él ______________________________

## Composición de una historia

Completa el inicio de la historia con detalles sustentatorios.

Martín estaba en el centro de pintura. Primero, él ______________________________

Objetivo: Escribir detalles para sustentar la oración temática.

## Writing a Story

Complete the story starter with supporting details.

The monarch butterfly is a beautiful insect. It is ______________________

## Writing a Story

Complete the story starter with supporting details.

The beaver is a very busy forest animal. Every day in the spring

Skill: Writing Details to Support a Topic Sentence

## Composición de una historia

Completa el inicio de la historia con detalles sustentatorios.

La mariposa monarca es un insecto muy hermoso. Es ____________

---

## Composición de una historia

Completa el inicio de la historia con detalles sustentatorios.

El castor es un animal del bosque que siempre está ocupado. En la primavera, todos los días él ____________

Objetivo: Escribir detalles para sustentar la oración temática.

## Writing a Story

Complete the story starter with supporting details.

Justin traveled to outer space in a rocket ship. He went ____________________

______________________________

______________________________

______________________________

______________________________

______________________________

______________________________

______________________________

---

## Writing a Story

Complete the story starter with supporting details.

It was tree planting day at school. First, Brittany and Jordan ____________________

______________________________

______________________________

______________________________

______________________________

______________________________

______________________________

______________________________

______________________________

Skill: Writing Details to Support a Topic Sentence.

## Composición de una historia

Completa el inicio de la historia con detalles sustentatorios.

Juan viajó al espacio exterior en una nave espacial. Fue a ____________________

______________________________________________

______________________________________________

______________________________________________

______________________________________________

______________________________________________

______________________________________________

______________________________________________

______________________________________________

## Composición de una historia

Completa el inicio de la historia con detalles sustentatorios.

Era el día de siembra de árboles en la escuela. Primero, Beatriz y José ____________

______________________________________________

______________________________________________

______________________________________________

______________________________________________

______________________________________________

______________________________________________

______________________________________________

______________________________________________

______________________________________________

Objetivo: Escribir detalles para sustentar la oración temática.

# Respuestas/Answer Key

**Page 6: What's the Main Idea?**

- **A)** A mother black bear spends two years training her cubs.
- **B)** On the way to school I saw many signs of spring.
- **C)** Beside Mr. White's boat house by the Salmon River, a mother mallard had built a large nest.
- **D)** Last Saturday it rained all day and my little sister and I had to stay in the house.
- **E)** Today, I painted a picture of a strange dream that I had last night.
- **F)** Emily had a secret hiding place in her house.

**Página 7: ¿Cuál es la idea principal?**

- **A)** Una osa negra madre dedica dos años de su vida en adiestrar a sus crías.
- **B)** Cuando iba camino a la escuela vi muchas señales del advenimiento de la primavera.
- **C)** Al lado del cobertizo del Sr. Pérez en el Río Salmón, una mamá pato había construido un gran nido.
- **D)** El sábado pasado llovió todo el día y mi hermanita y yo tuvimos que quedarnos en casa.
- **E)** Hoy hice un dibujo de un sueño muy extraño que tuve anoche.
- **F)** Emilia tenía un lugar secreto donde esconderse en su casa.

**Page 8: What's the Main Idea?**

- **A)** On Saturday morning I looked out the window and saw snowflakes dancing about.
- **B)** The barn mice were having a problem with the farmer's cat.
- **C)** The maple tree only grows in North America.
- **D)** Earthworms are very small animals.
- **E)** There are many kinds of trolls.
- **F)** A spider web is made of silk by the female spider.

**Página 9: ¿Cuál es la idea principal?**

- **A)** El sábado en la mañana miré por la ventana y vi que caían copos de nieve.
- **B)** Los ratones del establo tenían un problema con el gato del granjero.
- **C)** El árbol de arce sólo crece en América del Norte.
- **D)** Las lombrices de tierra son unos animales muy pequeños.
- **E)** Existen muchos tipos de duendes.
- **F)** La tela de araña está hecha de una seda elaborada por la araña hembra.

**Page 10: What is the Topic Sentence?**

1. Hockey is a good game to play.
2. Picking apples is fun.
3. The wind likes to play tricks in the fall.
4. Goldfish are easy to look after.

**Página 11: ¿Cuál es la oración temática?**

1. El hockey es un juego entretenido.
2. Recolectar manzanas es divertido.
3. Al viento le gusta jugarnos trucos en el otoño.
4. Los peces son fáciles de cuidar.

**Page 12: What is the Topic Sentence?**

1. A skunk is about the size of a house cat.
2. A raccoon uses its paws like a person.
3. The chickadee is a tiny gray bird.
4. Once there was an old school bus.

**Página 13: ¿Cuál es la oración temática?**

1. El zorrillo es casi del tamaño de un gato.
2. El mapache utiliza sus patas como si fuera una persona.
3. El paro es un ave pequeñita de color gris.
4. Había una vez un viejo autobús escolar.

**Page 16: Supporting Details**

- **A)** My dog can run fast.
- **B)** The trees lose their leaves.
- **C)** I took my dog for a long walk.
- **D)** We enjoyed watching the beavers cutting down the trees.
- **E)** Crows like to eat corn.
- **F)** Fluffy was Betty's pet kitten.

**Página 17: Detalles sustentatorios**

- **A)** Mi perro también puede correr rápido.
- **B)** Los árboles pierden sus hojas.
- **C)** Llevé a mi perro a dar un largo paseo.
- **D)** Disfrutamos ver a los castores cortando los árboles.
- **E)** A los cuervos les gusta comer maíz.
- **F)** Minino era el gatito de Beatriz.

**Page 22: Sequencing Sentences**

**A)** 4, 2, 1, 3 **B)** 2, 4, 1, 3 **C)** 3, 2, 4, 1

**Página 23: Oraciones de enlace**

**A)** 4, 2, 1, 3 **B)** 2, 4, 1, 3 **C)** 3, 2, 4, 1

**Page 24: Sequencing Sentences**

**A)** The robins were very busy building a nest of twigs and grass. Mother Robin laid three blue eggs in the nest. She sat on the eggs to keep them warm. Soon three baby robins hatched from the eggs.

**B)** Paul's alarm clock rang and woke him up. He got up and dressed quickly. Then he ate his breakfast. Finally, Paul was on his way to school.

**Página 25: Oraciones de enlace**

**A)** Los petirrojos estaban muy ocupados construyendo su nido con ramitas y pasto. La Mamá Petirrojo dejó tres huevos azules en el nido. Se sentó sobre los huevos para mantenerlos calientes. En poco tiempo, salieron tres petirrojos bebés de los cascarones.

**B)** La alarma de Pablo sonó y él se despertó. Se levantó y se vistió rápidamente. Luego tomó desayuno. Finalmente, Pablo se puso de camino a la escuela.